James A.
92 GAR

Joseph, P

D1034414

United States Presidents

James A. Garfield

Paul Joseph
ABDO Publishing Company

visit us at
www.abdopub.com

Published by ABDO Publishing Company 4940 Viking Drive, Edina, Minnesota 55435.
Copyright © 2000 by Abdo Consulting Group, Inc. International copyrights reserved in all countries. No part of this book may be reproduced in any form without written permission from the publisher.

Published 2000
Printed in the United States of America
Second Printing 2002

Photo credits: Archive Photos, UPI/Corbis-Bettmann

Contributing editors: Robert Italia, Tamara L. Britton, K.M. Brielmaier, Kate A. Furlong

Library of Congress Cataloging-in-Publication Data

Joseph, Paul, 1970-
    James A. Garfield / Paul Joseph.
       p. cm. -- (United States presidents)
    Includes index.
   Summary: A biography of the man who reluctantly became the twentieth president of the United States in 1881, only to be assassinated after just four months in office.
  ISBN 1-57765-242-8
  1. Garfield, James A. (James Abram), 1831-1881--Juvenile literature. 2. Presidents--United States--Biography--Juvenile literature. [1. Garfield, James A. (James Abram), 1831-1881. 2. Presidents.] I. Title. II. Series: United States presidents (Edina, Minn.)
E687.J824   1999
973.8'4'092--dc21
  [B]   98-19316
                                             CIP
                                           AC

Contents

James A. Garfield

*J*ames A. Garfield devoted most of his life to public service. He was a respected teacher and college president. He served in the Ohio senate, the U.S. **House of Representatives**, and the U.S. Senate.

Garfield studied hard in school and went to college. When the **Civil War** began, Garfield volunteered to fight for the North. From there he began his career in politics.

Garfield became president in 1881. Just four months later, he was shot in the back. After months of suffering, he died.

James A. Garfield

James A. Garfield (1831-1881)
Twentieth President

BORN:	November 19, 1831
PLACE OF BIRTH:	Orange Township, Ohio
ANCESTRY:	English, Huguenot
FATHER:	Abram Garfield (1799-1833)
MOTHER:	Eliza Ballou Garfield (1801-1888)
WIFE:	Lucretia Rudolph (1832-1918)
CHILDREN:	Seven: 5 boys, 2 girls
EDUCATION:	Geauga Academy, Western Reserve Eclectic Institute, Williams College
RELIGION:	Disciples of Christ
OCCUPATION:	Lawyer, soldier, professor, president of Western Reserve Eclectic Institute
MILITARY SERVICE:	Commissioned lieutenant colonel of 42nd Ohio Volunteers (1861), brigadier general (1862), major general (1863)

POLITICAL PARTY:	Republican
OFFICES HELD:	Ohio state senator, member of U.S. House of Representatives, chairman of the Committee of Appropriations, and minority leader
AGE AT INAUGURATION:	49
YEARS SERVED:	1881
VICE PRESIDENT:	Chester A. Arthur
DIED:	September 19, 1881, Elberon, New Jersey, age 49
CAUSE OF DEATH:	Assassination

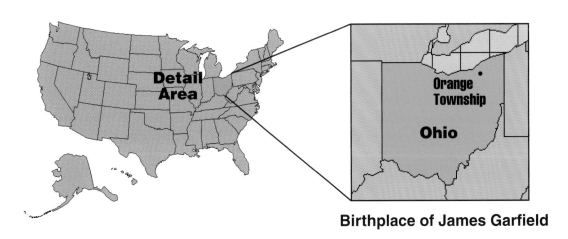

Birthplace of James Garfield

Young James

*J*ames Abram Garfield was born in Orange Township, Ohio, on November 19, 1831. His parents, Abram and Eliza, owned a farm. When James was only two years old, his father died.

Eliza took over the farm to keep her family together. She sold some of the land to get money to run the farm. The smaller farm was easier to handle. She also did sewing and weaving work for the neighbors.

James was the youngest of the Garfield's four surviving children. He had one brother, Thomas, and two sisters, Mehitabel and Mary. James and his brother helped their mother with farm chores.

When James was 15, he began working for neighbors. He chopped wood, washed sheep, and worked in the fields.

In 1848, James worked as a mule driver on a canal boat. The boat carried copper ore from Cleveland to Pittsburgh and returned with coal.

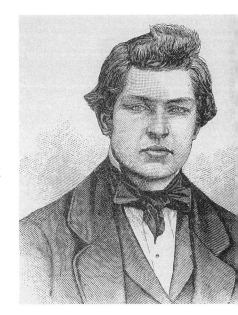

James Garfield as a young man

James daydreamed as he drove the mules along the canal. Since he was not paying attention, he often fell into the canal. He could not swim, and he almost drowned several times. After about six weeks of working on the canal, he caught **malaria**. He was sick for five months.

When James got better, Mrs. Garfield urged him to go to school. He agreed to give school a chance for one year before returning to the canal.

Off to School

*M*rs. Garfield knew that to do well in life James needed an education. She was happy that James was going to school. To start him off she gave him seventeen dollars. It was her life savings.

James enrolled at Geauga Academy. It was only 12 miles from home. While going to school, he earned extra money doing carpentry and other odd jobs. He also taught grade school during his term breaks.

James was an excellent student. He studied and worked hard. He no longer wanted to return to the canal. He wanted to continue his education at a better school.

For a year, James worked at odd jobs to earn money to stay in school. In 1851, he enrolled at Western

Reserve Eclectic Institute. At first, he paid his way working as a janitor.

At the Eclectic Institute, he studied more challenging subjects like algebra and Latin. He discovered he was good at public speaking and learned to debate.

By 1854, James had learned all he could at the Eclectic Institute. He started teaching there full time.

James wanted to continue his education in the East. He wanted to have new experiences beyond Ohio and the small schools he had attended.

In 1854, James entered Williams College in Williamstown, Massachusetts. He was a star debater and a good student. He was elected president of the Philogian Society, a literary club. He was editor of the *Williams Quarterly*. On August 7, 1856, he graduated with honors.

James and Lucretia

*G*arfield returned to Ohio to teach again at the Eclectic Institute. Less than a year later, he was elected school president.

In 1858, Garfield married Lucretia Rudolph. Her father was a **trustee** of the Eclectic Institute. The couple had a long and happy marriage. They had five sons, Harry, James, Irvin, Abram, and Edward. They also had two daughters, Eliza and Mary.

Lucretia was a well-educated woman. She was a member of many different clubs and did a lot of volunteer work throughout her lifetime. She also raised seven children while Garfield was away working.

While teaching, Garfield studied law on his own. He made excellent speeches for the new **Republican** party. The Republicans thought he would make a good leader.

Garfield ran for the Ohio senate in 1858, and was easily elected. He fought to end slavery in the South. He also fought against cutting funds for school libraries. He worked for Abraham Lincoln's presidential campaign in 1860. In 1861, he passed the bar examination and became a lawyer.

Lucretia Garfield

Civil War Officer

*T*he **Civil War** between the North and the South began in 1861. Garfield was ready to serve the Union. The governor of Ohio named him **lieutenant colonel** of the 42nd Ohio Volunteer Infantry.

Garfield **recruited** many people, including some of his former students. Company A of the 42nd Ohio was made up of students from the Eclectic Institute. Garfield began studying military **tactics**.

On January 10, 1862, Garfield's men were sent to Middle Creek in Kentucky. Kentucky was on the border between the North and South. It was **neutral** in the war. But the South invaded Kentucky to gain an advantage over the North. Garfield's men won a battle at Middle Creek that forced the South to retreat. Because of his victory, Garfield was made **brigadier general**.

On September 2, 1862, the people of Ohio elected Garfield to the U.S. **House of Representatives**. He would not take his political office until the following year.

In 1863, Garfield was named chief-of-staff to General William S. Rosecrans. Garfield saw action at the battles of Shiloh and Chickamauga. For his courage and leadership, he was rewarded with the rank of **major general**.

General Garfield

15

The Making of the Twentieth United States President

 **1831**

Born November 19 in Orange Township, Ohio

 **1833**

Father dies

 **1848**

Gets a job on a canal boat; catches malaria

 **1854**

Begins teaching at the Eclectic Institute; transfers to Williams College

 **1856**
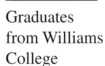

Graduates from Williams College

 **1861**
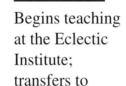

Civil War begins; appointed lieutenant colonel by Ohio governor

 **1862**
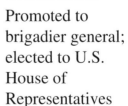
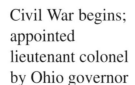

Promoted to brigadier general; elected to U.S. House of Representatives

James A. Garfield

"Next in importance to freedom and justice is popular education, without which neither freedom nor justice can be permanently maintained."

 **1848**

Enters Geauga Academy

 **1851**

Attends Western Reserve Eclectic Institute

Historic Events
during Garfield's Presidency

Russian Czar Alexander II is assassinated

First elevator installed in the White House

Auguste Rodin sculpts *The Thinker*

 **1858**

Marries Lucretia Rudolph; elected to Ohio senate

 **1861**

Passes bar exam and becomes a lawyer

1880

Elected to U.S. Senate; nominated for president and wins

1881

Begins civil service reform; shot by assassin July 2; dies September 19

PRESIDENTIAL YEARS

Garfield Goes to Washington

*A*lthough the North and South were still at war, President Lincoln asked Garfield to leave his military post and take his seat in **Congress**. In December of 1863, he went to Washington, D.C.

During his years in Congress, Garfield served on the Military Affairs Committee. He also served on the Ways and Means and Appropriations Committees.

During the **Civil War**, he fought against the commutation law. This law allowed men to get out of military service by paying the government $300. He fought for equal rights for African Americans.

Garfield was a leader in establishing the U.S. Department of Education. He helped create the U.S. Geological Survey. And he was a **regent** of the Smithsonian Institution.

After the war, Garfield became a **radical Republican**. He wanted a strong **Reconstruction** policy for the South. He supported the **impeachment** of President Andrew Johnson.

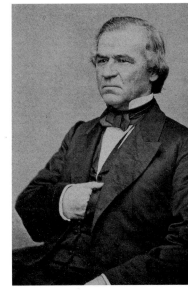

Andrew Johnson

Before 1913, senators were not elected by the people but were chosen by state **legislatures**. Early in 1880, the Ohio legislature elected Garfield to the U.S. Senate.

Garfield was excited about becoming a senator. But before he could join the Senate, he was nominated for president.

The Twentieth President

*J*ames A. Garfield went to the 1880 **Republican National Convention** to nominate Senator John Sherman for president. After Garfield gave his nominating speech, someone in the audience yelled, "We want Garfield!"

But Garfield did not want to be president. At one point, he jumped up and protested that he was not a candidate.

On the thirty-sixth **ballot**, Garfield was nominated. The entire audience stood and cheered. Garfield felt honored. He was ready to lead the country.

In November 1880, James A. Garfield was elected the twentieth president of the United States. He beat

Democratic candidate Winfield Scott Hancock by only 9,464 popular votes.

Garfield was sworn in as president on March 4, 1881. In his **inaugural** speech, he promised **civil service** reform. In the past, politicians had rewarded their supporters with civil service jobs. This was called the spoils system.

Garfield decided that he would not reward friends or supporters with civil service jobs. He believed in choosing the most qualified person for a job.

President Garfield's decision upset many of his fellow **Republicans** who were hoping to get civil service jobs.

President Garfield

Garfield complained in his diary that people were always pestering him for jobs. He began supporting a **civil service** reform law. This law would require people to take tests to see if they were qualified for certain civil service jobs.

During this time, there was a problem in the post office. In the West, there was no regular postal delivery. Contracts were awarded to private individuals to deliver the mail. Some people were charging the government more money than their contracts said they could.

President Garfield appointed Postmaster General Thomas James to investigate the problem. By June 1882, there was enough **evidence** for Attorney General Wayne McVeagh to **prosecute** the offenders. But the jury could not agree on a decision. The men on trial were set free.

The labels on the map read:
- Existing Territory
- Existing Territories
- Existing States
- Existing States

The United States during Garfield's presidency

The Seven "Hats" of the U.S. President

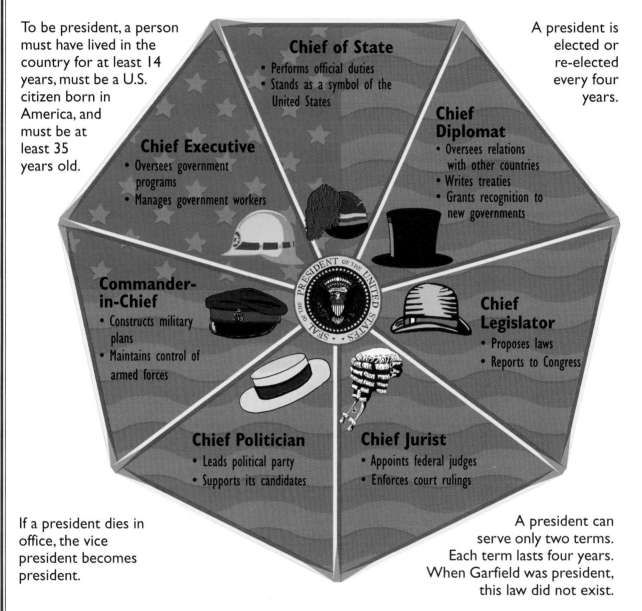

To be president, a person must have lived in the country for at least 14 years, must be a U.S. citizen born in America, and must be at least 35 years old.

A president is elected or re-elected every four years.

Chief of State
- Performs official duties
- Stands as a symbol of the United States

Chief Diplomat
- Oversees relations with other countries
- Writes treaties
- Grants recognition to new governments

Chief Executive
- Oversees government programs
- Manages government workers

Commander-in-Chief
- Constructs military plans
- Maintains control of armed forces

Chief Legislator
- Proposes laws
- Reports to Congress

Chief Politician
- Leads political party
- Supports its candidates

Chief Jurist
- Appoints federal judges
- Enforces court rulings

If a president dies in office, the vice president becomes president.

A president can serve only two terms. Each term lasts four years. When Garfield was president, this law did not exist.

As president, James Garfield had seven jobs.

The Three Branches of the U.S. Government

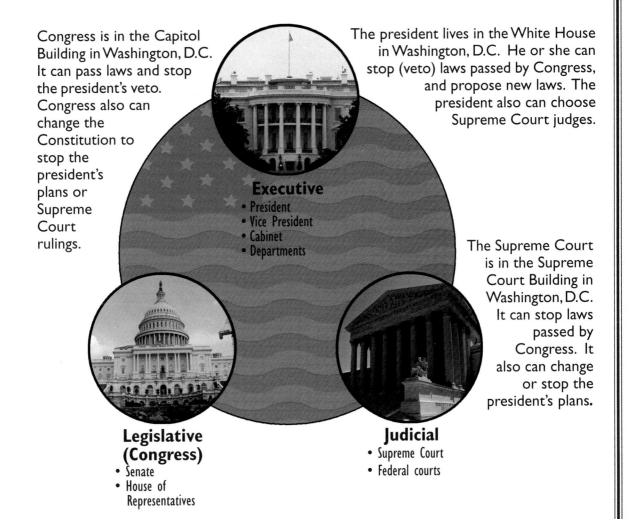

Congress is in the Capitol Building in Washington, D.C. It can pass laws and stop the president's veto. Congress also can change the Constitution to stop the president's plans or Supreme Court rulings.

The president lives in the White House in Washington, D.C. He or she can stop (veto) laws passed by Congress, and propose new laws. The president also can choose Supreme Court judges.

Executive
- President
- Vice President
- Cabinet
- Departments

The Supreme Court is in the Supreme Court Building in Washington, D.C. It can stop laws passed by Congress. It also can change or stop the president's plans.

Legislative (Congress)
- Senate
- House of Representatives

Judicial
- Supreme Court
- Federal courts

The U.S. Constitution formed three government branches. Each branch has power over the others. So, no single group or person can control the country. The Constitution calls this "separation of powers."

A Tragic Ending

*O*n the morning of July 2, 1881, President Garfield was in the Pennsylvania Railroad Station in Washington, D.C. He was going on vacation.

As Garfield waited for a train, a man approached him from behind and fired two shots. One bullet hit Garfield in the back. The shooter was Charles Guiteau. He was angry because Garfield would not give him a **civil service** job.

As Guiteau fired the shots, he shouted, "I am a Stalwart! [Vice President Chester] Arthur is president now!" The Stalwarts were a group of **Republicans** who opposed civil service reform. They believed in the spoils system. Vice President Arthur supported the Stalwarts.

Guiteau thought the Stalwarts would see him as a hero and give him a job. Instead, he was arrested and brought to trial. Guiteau was found guilty and soon hanged. President Garfield lived for nearly three months after the shooting. He died on September 19, 1881.

Garfield served his country most of his life. He believed in working hard, the value of education, and fighting for what he believed in. President Garfield was buried in Cleveland, Ohio.

James A. Garfield is wounded by Charles Guiteau.

Fun Facts

- James A. Garfield was the United States' first left-handed president.

- At the 1880 **Republican National Convention**, Garfield didn't receive a single vote on the first ballot.

- Although Garfield was considered left-handed, he could write perfectly with both hands. For fun, he would write in Greek with the right hand and in Latin with the left hand—at the same time!

- The public was so concerned about Garfield's family after his death that they donated more than $300,000.

- James A. Garfield was the last president born in a log cabin.

- President Garfield had the second shortest term as president in the history of the United States.

James Garfield

Glossary

assassinate - to murder a very important person.

ballot - when people cast votes.

brigadier general - a one-star general.

civil service - the part of the government that runs matters not covered by the military, the courts, or laws.

Civil War - a war between the Union and the Confederate States of America from 1861 to 1865.

Congress - the lawmaking body of the United States. It is made up of the Senate and the House of Representatives.

Democrat - a political party. When Garfield was president, they supported farmers and landowners.

evidence - proof.

House of Representatives - a group of people elected by citizens to represent them. They meet in Washington, D.C., and make laws for the country.

impeach - to have a trial to decide if the president should be removed from office.

inauguration - when a person is sworn into office.

legislature - a group of people elected by the citizens of the state to represent them and make laws. When Garfield was president, each state's legislature also elected its state senators.

lieutenant colonel - a military rank above a major and below a colonel.

major general - a military rank above a brigadier general; also, a two-star general.

malaria - a disease spread by mosquitoes that causes chills and fever.

neutral - not taking sides in a fight.

prosecute - to bring before a court of law.

radical - extreme.

Reconstruction - the period of time after the Civil War when laws were passed to help the Southern states rebuild, and return to the Union.

recruit - to gather people together for a task.

regent - a member of a governing board.

Republican - a political party. When Garfield was president, they supported business and strong government.

Republican National Convention - a national meeting held every four years during which the Republican party chooses its candidates for president and vice president.

tactics - the study of battle plans.

trustee - someone who supervises business matters.

Internet Sites

United States Presidents Information Page
http://historyoftheworld.com/soquel/prez.htm
Links to information about United States presidents. This site is very informative, with biographies on every president as well as speeches and debates, and other links.

The Presidents of the United States of America
http://www.whitehouse.gov/WH/glimpse/presidents/html/presidents.html
This site is from the White House. With an introduction from President Bill Clinton and biographies that include each president's inaugural address, this site is excellent. Get information on White House history, art in the White House, first ladies, first families, and much more.

POTUS—Presidents of the United States
http://www.ipl.org/ref/POTUS/
In this resource you will find background information, election results, cabinet members, presidency highlights, and some odd facts on each of the presidents. Links to biographies, historical documents, audio and video files, and other presidential sites are also included to enrich this site.

These sites are subject to change. Go to your favorite search engine and type in United States presidents for more sites.

Pass It On

History enthusiasts: educate readers around the country by passing on information you've learned about presidents or other important people who have changed history. Share your little-known facts and interesting stories. We want to hear from you!

To get posted on the ABDO Publishing Company Web site, email us at:
history@abdopub.com
Visit the ABDO Publishing Company Web site at www.abdopub.com

Index